DEAR JELLY

Family letters from the First World War

By Sarah Ridley

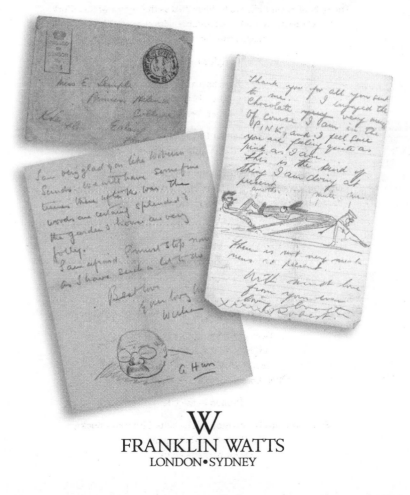

W
FRANKLIN WATTS
LONDON•SYDNEY

Eileen (Jelly)
and Mabel

Mabel, Mother and
Eileen (Jelly)

William, Mother, Noel
and Robert

William, Maud and Robert

THE SEMPLE FAMILY

Sir David Semple (born in 1856) ┬ Lady Ethel Semple (born in 1866)

William	Robert	Mabel	Noel
born in 1894	born in 1896	born in 1901	born in 1903, died in 1912

Maud	John	Eileen
born in 1895	born in 1899, died in 1900	(nickname 'Jelly') born in 1902

Sir David Semple was a leading doctor with the Royal Army Medical Corps. He was knighted (became Sir David Semple) in 1911 for his work with public health in India, including the introduction of the new rabies vaccine. Between 1913 and 1918 he was Director General of Public Health in Egypt, then under British occupation.

Lady Ethel Semple was Sir David's wife and mother to their seven children. Two of their sons died in childhood – John as a one-year-old and Noel of meningitis when he was eight.

Robert and William sit on the ground in this photo taken in 1907. Left to right: Eileen (Jelly), Noel and Mabel are wearing white coats. Their mother (Lady Semple) is sitting down. The nanny is standing with Maud to the right of her.

ᵛ AUGUST 1914 ᵛ

In August 1914 war broke out across Europe. Tensions
between countries had been building for some time.
Almost all the countries of Europe were linked together
by agreements to support each other in the case of attack
or invasion. It took the assassination of Archduke Franz
Ferdinand, heir to the Austrian throne, to start a chain of
reactions that brought country after country into war.
On 4 August, Britain declared war on Germany, joining
forces with France and Russia against Germany and
Austria-Hungary.

In August 1914, William and Robert Semple and a school
friend were on a walking holiday in Bavaria, Germany. The
outbreak of war took them by surprise and they had to find
a safe route home. Picking up Maud, their sister, from a
finishing school at a convent in Bavaria on the way, they fled
across France alongside refugees who were escaping in front
of the German advance. They eventually arrived home on a
steamboat.

Home was a house in Ealing, a suburb of London. There
were five Semple children: William 19, Maud 18, Robert 17,
Mabel 13 and Eileen 12. William and Robert had nicknames
for their youngest sisters: Mabel they called 'Suet' and Eileen
'Jelly'. In 1914, Mabel and Eileen were just about to go away
to boarding school for the first time. Up until then they had
been educated at home, taught by a governess.

William was due to return to Cambridge University where he was studying to become a doctor like his father. Instead he joined the army and in 1915, after completing his officer training, he left for France as a Second Lieutenant in the King's Royal Rifle Corps.

His younger brother, Robert, persuaded his parents to let him join the Royal Military Academy, Woolwich, to train as an officer in the artillery. In July 1915 he left Woolwich and joined the Royal Field Artillery. Like his brother, he was sent to France to fight on the Western Front.

To keep in touch with home, William and Robert wrote letters. Their sisters kept many of these letters and they have been passed down to the next generation.

~ 1914/1915 ~

William drew this picture
of himself in a letter to
his sister Eileen.

By the time William Semple arrived in France in 1915, the war had been going for almost a year.

At the beginning, the German army took over large areas of Belgium and parts of France. The French and British armies fought back, most notably at the Battle of the Marne, slowing down the German advance. However, by November 1914 the war had ground to a halt. The use of field guns, firing huge numbers of shells one after the other, made open warfare extremely difficult. So both armies now rushed to build trenches which stretched from the Swiss border to the Belgium coast.

Back in Britain, the army had launched a massive recruitment campaign. Its army was also expanding due to a flood of soldiers from countries in the Commonwealth including Canada, Australia, New Zealand and India. The fighting took place across the world: on the Western Front (France/Belgium), the Eastern Front (Russia), in the Balkans, Africa and the Middle East.

During 1915, trench warfare continued with small skirmishes, trench raids and bombardments, as well as battles. The German army used poison gas for the first time against the British in April 1915 when they attacked the British front line close to Ypres in Belgium. The British used it against the Germans in September of that same year, at the beginning of the Battle of Loos.

Thousands of men lost their lives during 1915 in France and Belgium, as well as on other battlefronts. The British were particularly badly affected during the Battle of Loos in September: around 60,000 British soldiers died, were injured or taken prisoner, as compared to only about 20,000 German soldiers.

In the spring of 1915, William Semple, who sometimes signed himself as Bill, wrote these letters to his sisters. They were both at Princess Helena's College, Ealing, a private boarding school for girls. Mabel was 13 and Eileen 12.

My dear Mabel,

Thanks awfully for your very amusing letters. I must congratulate you on your gym distinctions – I shall expect to find you something like this when I come home.

Look at all the medals for gymnastics!

I hope you have a good time when you are home for the Easter hols. I expect this letter will find you there. Don't behave like the girl in the limerick:

There once was a girl of St Helena's,
Who really was getting on well in years,
She ate so much pudden (pudding)
That all of a sudden
She burst – and her poor mother fell in tears.

Sorry to have to write such a short note but time presses.

Best love
Bill.

Picture of time pressing and my sorrow.

Bill doesn't describe his own life but he must have been training as an officer at this time. Officers learnt how to lead and give orders, as well as follow them. They also learnt fighting skills, battle tactics, map reading, basic first aid and how to dig trenches.

Eileen's brothers often called her Jelly, using a family nickname linked to her love of the dessert, jelly.

Dear Jelly,

Thanks awfully for all your very amusing letters. I must congratulate you on your gym distinctions but I won't draw a picture of you as I have just drawn one for Mabel. Instead I am drawing a picture of a rabbit – so that you can add it to your stock of useful knowledge.

I hope you have a jolly time during the Easter holidays.

I have written Mabel a piece of poetry so I must do the same for you.

Ode to a Rabbit

Why does my bunny
Look so funny?
It makes me cry
Because I try
With all my might
To draw it right.
But when I say, "see! That's some bunny,"
They always laugh and say, "How funny!"

I must draw one more picture to make your letter equal to Mabel's. Why not a picture of myself?

Best love
Bill

William sketches himself in uniform, performing a salute. His army rank of second lieutenant is shown by the symbol on his shoulder strap. Bill clearly loved receiving letters with news from home. If all went smoothly, letters and parcels could reach soldiers in France within two days of being posted in Britain. Sometimes it took much longer, especially if the soldier was on the move.

Midway through the year, the family moved house from Ealing to Woburn Sands, a village close to modern-day Milton Keynes. In August, Mabel was enjoying the summer holidays when she received this letter from William. He seems to have spent a few days on leave at the new family home before he left for France. Military records show that his battalion of the King's Royal Rifle Corps arrived in France on 30 July 1915. By this time, both sides had been fighting for almost a year in a war that had quickly become bogged down in trench warfare.

William teases Mabel about how lovely (in fact awful) it would be if her rather terrifying headmistress, Miss Parker, came to stay. Miss Parker was friendly with Mabel's mother, who was a governor of the school.

13th K.RR.C.   14th Aug
37th Division
B.E.F. France

My dear Mabel,

I am enclosing a postal order for you and Eileen. I have to change them for my men and as it is no use sending small ones to the bank and they can't be changed at the French Post Office, I will send them home to you and Eileen whenever I get any.

Isn't the house ripping, and what do you think of the woods at Woburn Sands? I am sure you would be delighted to have Miss Parker to stay at "Sandymount". I hope she makes you eat all the meat and beats you hard every day first to keep you up to the mark now your brothers are away.

We have to do an enormous lot of marching under a very heavy pack.

The above illustrates the real and the supposed way in which a soldier marches. No I is the real way and no II is the way he ought to march.

We expect to go to the trenches next week so look out for parcels of German scalps and van loads of helmets etc.

Best love
Your loving brother
William

William's drawings show the uniform quite clearly – the stiff
cloth cap, the wool tunic, trousers and puttees. These were long
strips of cloth that soldiers wound around their legs over wool
socks and the bottom of their short trousers. The wide belt had
pouches for ammunition and tools. The large pack contained a
long coat and a blanket – the coat alone weighed 6 lb (almost
3 kg). Officers were allowed to carry a walking stick. William
was clearly feeling hot in all this uniform – it was the summer.

Eileen received this next letter around her 13th birthday in
early October 1915. William contrasts his living quarters in
the trenches with those at a rest camp set back from the front
line. He appears to be missing home and would rather be
there than out in France.

13th KRRC
B.E.F. France

My dear Eileen,

Many happy returns of the day. I hope you will spend a
pleasant birthday amid the prim, scholastic atmosphere of
P.H.C. [Princess Helena's College]. I must say I envy you being
in England at all although I dare say everyone at home wishes
they were out here – they wouldn't if they once tried it.

We are out of the trenches at present and don't expect to go back for a fortnight at least. I can't say that we are glad to be out of the trenches as they are very comfortable which is more than can be said for our present quarters. In the trenches we live in a comfortable "dug-out" – that is a hole in the ground with a good roof and a very comfortable bed. I had a chair and a table in my "dug-out" and several large cupboards and the whole place looked very nice and I was quite sorry to leave it when we were relieved.

Out of the trenches we do nothing but dig new lines of trenches all day and sometimes all night. The weather is still very hot and far from pleasant for digging in.

Every day we see several aeroplanes being shelled and yesterday there was a very exciting fight just over our heads – two English aeroplanes chased a Hun [German] plane firing hard all the time. To our intense disappointment they failed to bring him down.

Excuse this short note but I am awfully full up with work.

Best love

Your loving brother
William

William writes that he is out of the trenches at the moment. The trenches were parallel lines of ditches, usually following a zigzag route to provide extra defence against attack and protection from shell fire. The soil removed during the digging of the trench was piled up to form a mound of earth, running in front of the trench.

Groups of soldiers took it in turn to defend the front line trench from attack, spend time in the reserve trenches or be at rest. Over a period of five weeks, William and his men probably spent about two weeks in the front line, a week in a parallel support trench and two weeks in a reserve trench further behind that one. Finally they would spend about a week in a rest camp, set back from the action.

Often being 'at rest' meant digging more trenches, which William clearly did not enjoy. These may have been communication trenches, which ran at 90 degree angles to the main trenches. These trenches were used by soldiers to move between the lines and to carry supplies of food and ammunition up to the front line trenches. Often sandbags were added to all trenches to provide more protection from German attacks.

William writes fondly of his dugout, an underground shelter connected to a trench. Some officers had quite large dugouts, big enough for beds and tables. They provided added protection from exploding enemy shells as well as somewhere to sleep, eat and relax.

At the end of the letter William describes an air battle. At the beginning of the war the Royal Flying Corps had 63 aeroplanes in France. Gradually the number of planes increased and by 1918 the Royal Air Force (as it had become) had over 1,800 aeroplanes in France.

William's brother Robert arrived in France with the Royal Field Artillery in August 1915. During his training with the artillery, Robert had learnt how to work with the field guns (the artillery) and how to command the men needed to load and fire the shells. A couple of months after he arrived at the front line, Robert sent this serious letter to Mabel and Eileen describing a battle and the sudden death of a soldier. He sends his love twice over at the end, once from Bob (his family nickname), and once from Robert.

D Battery 76 Brigade
Guards Divisional Artillery
B.E.F. France   21st October 1915.

My dearest Mabel and Eileen,

Thanks very much for your letters. I should have answered them before but I have not had much time just lately for writing.

Well cheer oh! As you may guess, I have about twelve iron crosses and a string of medals. Anyway I have some nice souvenirs to bring back. We are not allowed to send parcels or I would send you some.

At present I am sitting in a trench a little way from the Germans smoking my new pipe and feeling very cold. Unfortunately writing letters does not make me sweat.

In the last few days we have had two big battles here and both times we took some more trenches.

While our troops were attacking, the guns had to fire away as hard as they could. The noise was terrible. There were thousands of guns all firing at the same time. All the horizon was one mass of smoke and bursting shells.

Here is a picture of what our battery looked like during the battles.

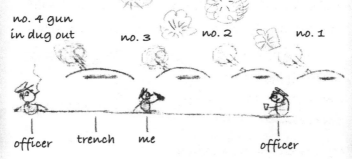

no. 4 gun in dug out   no. 3   no. 2   no. 1

officer   trench   me   officer

I often have to go up the trenches observing and they look an awful sight after a battle. They are all battered to pieces and full of dead men, English and Germans.

There are a lot of snipers round here The other day I was laying a wire down one of the trenches when I saw a soldier who was outside the trench get hit in the back. He sat down backwards and for a minute went on smoking his pipe as if nothing had happened. Suddenly he seemed to feel the pain. He dropped his pipe and let out a yell. Immediately three or four men jumped up to pull him into safety. Amongst them was a Sergeant Major. The minute the Sergeant Major got out of the trench he was shot through the heart. A piece of very bad luck.

We all live in dugouts here as there are no houses left standing anywhere near the firing trenches.

Each battalion in the firing line has several pigeons to carry messages using a bottle when the telephone wires have been cut by shells.

When I get some leave I will bring home all the souvenirs I can lay my hands on.

Write and let me know all your news for I love getting letters out here.

Well to make it quite fair here is a note for each of you.

> My dear Mabel
> Much love from Bob
> With much love from
> your ever loving brother
>
> Robert xxxxxxx

> My dear Eileen
> Much love from Bob
> With much love from
> your ever loving brother
> Robert xxxxxxx

Robert mentions souvenirs twice
in this letter. He has been collecting
German medals from the uniforms of
dead soldiers, or prisoners of war,
in order to send them home for
his little sisters. The Iron Cross
was a medal awarded for bravery
by the German army.

He describes the noise of a battle and being deafened by the
guns. Passing on orders to his men, Robert would have been
standing right beside the huge guns in his gun battery as they
fired off as many shells as possible at the German trenches. In
return, the Germans tried to destroy the British trenches and
their gun positions. The aim of both sides was to win battles
and claim land that had been held by the enemy.

Robert writes of trenches full of dead soldiers, German and
English, after an attack. This attack was part of the Battle
of Loos, which took place from 25 September to mid October
1915. About 43,000 British soldiers died or were injured
during the battle, the highest losses of the war until then.

Robert also describes a single death caused by a German
sniper. Perhaps he was shocked by how quickly the sergeant
major lost his own life when he came out of the trench to
rescue the other soldier. Robert had only been in France for a
few months at this time – and he was still only 19.

Robert mentions two ways that the different parts of the army kept in contact during the war. One was by laying basic telephone wires along the trenches. The other involved the use of homing pigeons, trained to carry messages back to command centres set back from the front lines.

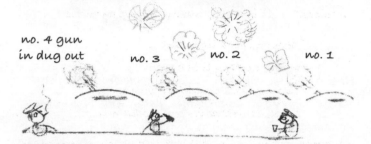

no. 4 gun
in dug out   no. 3   no. 2   no. 1

In Robert's sketch of "our battery", you can see four big guns, with their barrels pointing at the German front line. The guns fired shells, metal cases filled with explosives and shrapnel, balls of lead. Some shells contained gas.

A month later, Mabel and Eileen received a much more cheerful letter from Robert, even though he talks about what he and his brother will have written on their tombstones! William had already written a letter to his sisters about this morbid subject but it hasn't survived.

D/76 Guards Div(isional) Art(illery)   19/11/15
B.E.F. France

My dearest Mabel & Eileen,

The minute I received your letter and read what Bill was going to have on his tombstone I said to myself, "Good Gracious". This is what I intend to have on mine.

> "Robert was a little Sub
> Had a tummy like a tub
> But now he's covered up with earth
> So please restrain from ribald mirth."

We are in action again, but this is a much quieter place than the last one. Today I have been up observing. The observing post is a ruined house about a hundred yards from the firing line.

This is what I look like observing.

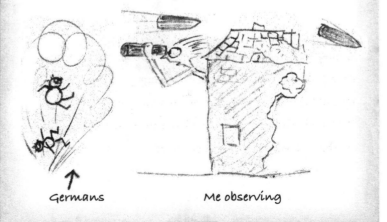

Germans   Me observing

The paper fancy dress ball must have been ripping.
I hope to get leave for a few days while Father is at home.

This is what I look like.

Me

Mud

This is what I want to look like.

Bad attempt

Another

Now you know everything there is to be known.
With much love from your ever loving brother
Robert x x x x x x x

Robert draws himself looking miserable in the French mud.
His division were positioned in a part of the front line where
the land was marshy, so the trenches would have been
particularly muddy.

"This is what I want to look like," Robert writes, drawing himself looking strong and in command with a German soldier begging for mercy at his feet. As an officer, he carried a revolver and a sword, which he shows dripping with German blood! Robert draws the other German soldier with a shell skimming the top of his spiked helmet, part of his uniform, and with an Iron Cross around his neck.

Earlier in the letter (see page 23), Robert mentions another part of his job as an officer in the Royal Field Artillery: "Today I have been up observing." Each side needed to work out where the enemy was entrenched and what the enemy was planning to do next by looking at the movements of soldiers in the opposite trenches. One way of doing this was to send men forward of the front line into observation posts, which could be wrecked buildings or even fake trees. The artillery in particular relied on information of this sort in order to work out where to aim their guns.

1916

In 1916, on the Western Front, the war was dominated by two long battles. Early in the year, in a bid to get the war moving again, the Germans made plans to capture the French fortress at Verdun. This battle began in February with a huge bombardment and lasted for months. The French army fought back but suffered terrible losses. By November about 370,000 French soldiers had died and about 350,000 Germans. Verdun remained in the hands of the French.

During the spring of 1916, the British army and her allies planned a huge attack along the German front line, close to the River Somme in France. They wanted to break the deadlock of months of trench warfare and help relieve pressure on the French, fighting at Verdun. The battle began on 1 July with a disastrous first day for the British, and continued until mid-November. Over a million lives were lost on both sides during the Battle of the Somme. At great cost, a strip of land 32 km (20 miles) long and 9.5 km (6 miles) deep was now in the hands of the British and her allies.

In the new year of 1916, William (Bill) thanked Mabel
and Eileen for sending out Christmas gifts for the men he
commanded. Eileen wrote a memoir at the end of her life
where she mentions that she spent time at school knitting
scarves, socks and balaclavas for the troops – but in this case,
the gifts were food.

3-1-16

My dear Mabel,

Thank you and Eileen and anyone else who was
responsible for sending out all these splendid Xmas
things for my men. It was with the greatest
difficulty I could refrain from eating them
myself, and my mouth watered like anything
when I saw all that you had sent. I hope you
had a jolly Xmas and thought of the poor flabby
Germans sitting in their trenches, weeping for
the absent sausages, wailing for their long-lost
beer mugs, and trembling at the thought of your
fierce brother waiting to shoot them the moment
they put their heads out of the trench.

How did you come off for Xmas presents?

I expect to get leave in about three weeks, but I am afraid you will be back at P.H.C. [Princess Helena's College] by then. We are not having a very comfortable time out here just now. The mud is as thick and plentiful as ever and it is great fun being dug out of it when one gets stuck there. I never really knew what mud was like until this winter. When I come home I shall be so pleased to escape from it that you will see me dancing about in the middle of the muddiest street in Woburn Sands simply chortling with joy.

I am afraid that as nothing seems to happen here I have nothing to tell you – so goodbye.
Happy New Year.

Best love
Bill

Bill would have liked to eat all the food gifts sent out by Mabel and Eileen to his men! Soldiers in the trenches longed for parcels of food sent from home since basic army rations of bully beef (tinned corned beef) and hardtack biscuits were very dull. The army did have mobile kitchens that cooked up big stews. Working parties carried the hot food in containers up to the men in the trenches when it was safe for them to do so.

Later the same month, Robert wrote to his sisters describing himself as "in the pink", meaning in good health. He confesses that he has written identical letters to the sisters by using a piece of carbon paper to create a copy.

No 1 Section

Guards DAC (Divisional Artillery Corps)

14th Jan. 1916

Oh my dearest Mabel/Eileen

I keep on having a fearful dread that you will discover my awful secret – But no. It is too late now, so I will go ahead with my dreadful work. I owe you each a letter so I am WRITING TO EACH OF YOU.

TWO LETTERS.   ah.

HA!   HA!

Thank you for all you sent to me. I enjoyed the chocolate very much. Of course I am in the PINK, and I feel sure you are feeling quite as pink as I am.

This is the kind of thing I am doing at present.

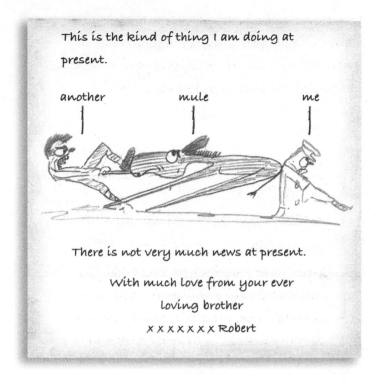

There is not very much news at present.

With much love from your ever
loving brother
x x x x x x Robert

As part of his job, Robert made sure that the mules and horses were well looked after. The artillery depended on horses and mules to pull the immensely heavy guns around, but the animals didn't always want to follow orders. At one point in 1917, the army was using almost a million horses and mules. About a third of them were ridden by the cavalry, the mounted troops, but the rest pulled guns, wagons or ambulances. The wagons carried supplies of food, ammunition, troops, tents and equipment.

Robert drew another picture of mules in his next letter.
Mabel must have been asking after them.

9.3.16

My dearest Mabel,

It is half past two, and I am sitting down with a cup of coffee and a cigarette after lunch to write this letter. At present we are billeted in a farm. It is quite a nice place. We are some distance from the firing line, having a rest. For the last few days there has been snow on the ground.

Just at present it is thawing and it is quite warm. There is not much news to tell you. All the mules are in the best of health.

I have just got two new ones in my section. They are both very old and fat.

They are very quiet.
Quite two little old gentlemen.

The Guards Divisional Artillery has been having a big boxing competition. The finals are this afternoon. One man from our section stands a very good chance of winning one of the prizes.

Give my love to Eileen. Tell her I will write to her soon.

Thanks for your letter.

With much love from your ever loving brother
Robert x x x x x x x

My address
2nd Lieut R Semple
No 1 Section
Guards D.A.C.
B.E.F.
Or No 1 Section
Guards Divisional Ammunition Column
B.E.F.

Robert was out of the front line having a rest when he wrote this letter. His billet is the army word for where he was sleeping. The army filled barns with bunk beds for soldiers to sleep on or simply spread straw on the floor. Billets could also be tents, half-ruined houses or villagers' homes. Wherever they were sleeping, these rest periods gave soldiers a chance to relax, have some fun – and wash themselves and their kit (uniform).

Eileen had obviously been writing plenty of letters to her brother William. He wrote that he is looking forward to spending time with her in the countryside after the war.

13th K.R.R.C.

B.E.F.

France

My dear Eileen,

I think that it is my turn to write to you as I wrote to Mabel last time. Thank you both so much for your numerous and very interesting letters – I always enjoy hearing from you. We have just come out of the trenches again. While I was there I managed to shoot at least one German who I met out at night in front of the trenches. I now feel very blood-thirsty and you will have to take care how you behave when I get back. If you tease me at all I shall whip out a revolver and bang! And then where will you be?

One of our officers – Captain Stocks – has got a sister at P.H.C. [Princess Helena's College] – a mistress – Miss Stocks. What sort is she – one of the Miss Parker [the scary headmistress] or the "whiskey" kind?

I expect you are just about to go back to school and are looking forward to it very much – (je ne pense pas). This last sentence is a sort of examination paper to see if you know your French.

I am very glad you like Woburn Sands. We will have some fine times there after the war. The woods are certainly splendid and the garden and house are very jolly.

I am afraid I must stop now as I have such a lot to do.

Best love

Your loving brother
William

A Hun

William writes about shooting a German whilst out on night patrol. Out in No Man's Land, the area of land between the German and British front line trenches, German and British soldiers alike crept about under cover of darkness. They laid down more barbed wire defences, brought back the dead or wounded, spied on the enemy and sometimes took prisoners back to their trenches.

At the end of June 1916, the Semple family received shattering news. William's commanding officer wrote them a letter saying that William was 'missing in action'. Time passed and this turned into 'missing, presumed dead'.

In the run up to the Battle of the Somme, William's commanding officer planned a trench raid to gather information and provide a distraction from where the British army was really going to attack along the front line. William was one of the four officers and 70 men of the King's Royal Rifle Corps who carried out this raid on 29 June. The raid did not go well and the men were forced to retreat. Sadly William was one of the men who failed to return.

Eventually, confirmation of William's death reached the family by a strange route. Through friends in the War Office, William's mother and aunt gained permission to question a German officer who had been captured and was now a prisoner of war in England. He had witnessed the raid carried out by William and his battalion, and had seen him lying dead in the trench. The German officer had identified him by a tailor's bill in his jacket pocket. The officer told William's mother that they had buried William, marking the grave with his name on a wooden cross. William was 21.

The Battle of the Somme had been planned for months. It lasted from July until November and involved both the French and the British armies. The aim was to break the deadlock of trench warfare and move the front line forward to a victory against the Germans.

It began with a week of heavy bombardment of the German trenches in the last week of June, in which Robert Semple's battery of guns took part. On 1 July, thousands of troops left the safety of their trenches to walk across No Man's Land. Although the Germans had suffered during the bombardment, many had survived in their deep trenches and now returned to their machine guns and mowed down the British soldiers walking towards them. On the first day of the battle, over 19,000 British soldiers were killed and almost 40,000 were injured.

The battle continued until November, in different phases, with little ground gained, but it did weaken the German army. Despite the tremendous number of soldiers who were killed or injured, some historians feel that, in its way, the battle helped to edge towards eventual victory in 1918.

After their brother's death, life was difficult at home for Mabel and Eileen. They felt a deep sadness while their mother was heartbroken and had a nervous breakdown.

Still, letters kept on coming from their remaining brother, Robert. In this one, dated 11 July, no mention is made of William's death. It seems likely that Robert hadn't heard the news yet.

11.7.16

My dearest Mabel and Jelly,

Best love to you both. I suppose by this time it is getting near the Summer Holidays. I hope I can get leave while you and Father are at home. I heard that Mother and Father and Maud went to see the play. Write and tell me all about it. It is so long since I wrote to you last. I am now in a trench MORTAR battery.

A trench mortar is a small gun which fires a large bomb from our trenches to the Huns. Of course this is all very nice and as it should be and of course we never forget to send our love with the bomb—

But the Huns also have a big mortar which also fires a big bomb from their trenches to ours.

Result

There are two officers in a battery and we take it in turns to go up to the trenches. We have a big dugout at the reserve billet and a small dugout up in the trenches – just big enough for one man to lie down in.

At the end of two days we change over. This is so that there should be one officer always up with the guns. We do this all the time we are in action.

I am in the best of health and I think of you all the time.

Write soon.

With much love from your

ever loving brother,

Robert xxxxxxx

My address – 2nd Lieut Semple

"Y" Guards Trench Mortar Battery.

The trench mortar that Robert describes here was a new type of weapon developed during the First World War. It was lighter than the big guns so it could be carried into position in the trenches. It launched shells in quick succession with the aim of destroying German gun positions and trenches – and killing as many German soldiers as possible. Robert served with the "Y" Guards Trench Mortar Battery from July 1916 until November 1918. A sketch that he made of his crew has survived.

Robert has drawn himself as the officer with the telescope, desperately looking for the correct target. In the foreground is a trench mortar shell, a canister of explosives with a fuse at the top. The crew have apparently grabbed one of their fellow soldiers and rammed him down the cylinder of the trench mortar instead of a shell.

By the time Robert wrote this next letter, he must have heard the bad news about William. He has taken a lot of care to fill the letter with drawings.

25th Sept. 1916

My dearest Mabel and Eileen,

How you must envy me. I don't have to go back to school for the Xmas term. Oh what joy! Think how nice it must be to sleep in a little dugout with a door and a bank.

My dugout

I have just been interrupted. A party of about eighty Hun prisoners marched by looking very cross and tired.

Note that most of them have lost their caps. I suspect they go as souvenirs rather early in the proceedings.

Still more prisoners are going by, so this letter is getting on very slowly. The last few days have been quite warm. I have been having a rest like this.

Plenty of little things happen out here to prevent life becoming dull. The other day I was sitting in a shell hole with another officer admiring the view when all of a sudden an 8-inch shell burst in the shell hole just behind us. The exciting part of these big shells is that you can always hear them coming, and you always think they are going to land bang onto you.

We were covered with dirt but otherwise none the worse.

See fig i & ii

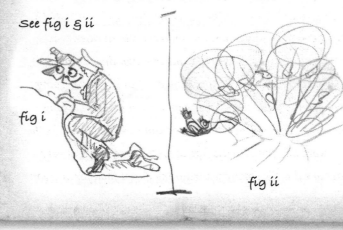

fig i

fig ii

I am in fine health, and the best of spirits.

Please write and tell me all the news.

Excuse a short letter.

With much love from

your ever loving brother

Robert xxxxxx

P.S. Thank you very much for your letters. I am very
pleased to get them.

Yours and tons of love from Bob

Robert describes the German prisoners as "cross and tired".
The moment of surrender, for soldiers on both sides, was
a difficult one. Many felt they had let down their country.
They would also have felt frightened about what was going
to happen to them next. Once captured, it could be a long
journey back from the front line to camps in England. As the
war wore on, British prisoners in German camps had very
little to eat as Germany was running out of food for everyone –
its army, prisoners and citizens alike.

In November 1916, Robert was in a rest camp and had time to send a letter full of cartoons to Mabel. He is obviously trying to make her laugh. He begins by asking her to raise a toast to herself and to Pie. 'Pie' might be Mabel's friend, Muriel de Paiva. He tells Mabel not to worry about their eldest sister, Maud, who has decided to become a nun. At the end of this letter he also draws a note for Jelly (Eileen).

Nov.3 1916

My dearest Mabel,
Here's to you, and here's another to Pie, and having acknowledged the toast, you will read as follows –

In the year 16 there lived a young fellow at a certain village (noted alike for the size of its shell holes and its fine natural water supply).

Now every morning this young fellow got up and every evening he went to bed, and this he did with great regularity and precision for a very considerable period.

And the other things that he did were to fire a trench mortar –

Bomb

Run very swiftly –

And live in a dugout, and so you can see for yourself what a very complete young fellow he was.

At present we are not in action. We are building huts, so do not worry about me. I do not worry on Maud's account for I can see nothing stranger in her mode of life than in any other.

Needless to say I am in the best of health.

Oh my best of love to you and to Eileen and heaps and heaps of kisses. From your ever loving brother Robert xxxxxxx.

The sketch at the bottom of this letter shows Robert waving to his sisters, standing on the top of a distant hill with the sea in between them.

~ 1917 ~

The war continued on all battlefronts in 1917. On the Western Front, a push forward planned by the French army ended in disaster and the mutiny of many of its soldiers.

On 6 April, the United States of America joined the war, against the Germans. It took several months for their soldiers and equipment to arrive.

On 31 July, the Third Battle of Ypres, also known as Passchendaele, began. Once again, the plan was for the British army and her allies to push their front line forward. There were some successes, especially when the British used tanks, but the weather was terrible. Heavy rain created mud and misery for all concerned. By 10 November, the Allies had pushed their front line forward a little. The battle left hundreds of thousands of men dead on both sides.

In the east, the Russian Revolution led eventually to the Russians agreeing an armistice with the Germans in mid December. The official peace treaty between the two countries was signed on 3 March, 1918.

In the spring of 1917, Lady Ethel brought a small boy called Sam into the household. Eileen wrote in her memoirs that her mother, Lady Ethel, had come across Sam in a home for illegitimate children. "The owner of the home... told mother that the father of the baby was an educated man who had been killed in the war." Lady Ethel also decided that the family should move house, again, this time to St Albans. Maybe the move led to letters being lost; few letters survive from 1917.

Eileen's memoirs say that Eileen and Mabel behaved badly about the toddler. "We were furious. We knew mother was trying to make up for the loss of Bill and Noel but the thought that this strange baby could take their place enraged us. Also we had to help look after him." Noel, their youngest brother, had died of a childhood illness in 1912, and Bill in the war (see page 36). The sisters were even less pleased when their mother agreed to care for another little boy called Tom. His mother had died and his father was fighting in the war.

In June Robert wrote to Mabel, hoping to see her soon and also worrying about his mother. As these two letters are undated, they may have been written in June 1916. Either way, Robert is hoping to see his family soon when he gets his next leave, the army word for time off.

June 4th

My dearest Mabel,

Let us hope that I can get a leave while you and Eileen are at home, but you cannot expect too much in the way of leaves just at present.

I am very glad you are going home, because Mother is getting older and she cannot work as she used to.

Lay in a good stock of wines, and a barrel or two of beer, and about two hundred bottles of whiskey, some old port, a keg of rum and some sloe gin and I think my visit ought to pass off quite well.

I think of you with dumbbells and Indian clubs figure marching all the day. I am also leading the active life. Sun baths every day with lots of pipes and long drinks.

I think your rabbit farm is quite a good idea and I hope it goes on well.

Give my best love to Eileen and tell her I will write soon.

Huns get troublesome at this time of the year, so I cannot write as often as I want to (I hope you believe that!).

With best love from your loving brother

Robert

Mabel told her own children that once, when Robert was on home leave, they were out walking together and she asked him to be honest about how he was feeling about his life as a soldier. He said, "It's the best thing I've ever done." We don't know whether he said this to reassure his sister that he could cope with life in the trenches, or whether he meant that he felt his role as a soldier was worthwhile.

Eileen must have laughed out loud when she read this next letter from her brother. Making light, as usual, of the danger he is in, he included a little song written in soldiers' slang, Anglo-French. These notes will help you understand it:

alleman – from the French word for 'a German'

Boshe – from the French word for 'rascal', used to describe German soldiers

crumping – the sound a German shell made as it exploded

pas bon – from the French for 'not good'

tres beans – *très bien* – from the French for 'very good'

June 11th

My dearest Eileen

The Hun is really a nasty man and I don't love him
any more after he drove me from my bed at 3.30 am the
other morning. I am glad you did not see me because
I am sure I did not look very noble tracking across
country in my pyjamas.

I felt so angry that I determined to do something that
would place the Boshe outside the pale for good and all so
I wrote this verse to the tune of John Peel.

> Alleman pas bon
> as I've oftimes said,
> When the sound of his crumping
> brought me from my bed.
> Alleman pas bon
> tres beans when he's dead
> When he crumps round my
> billet in the morning.

I am very well but I have very little news.

I live on a farm with a madame, her daughter, an old
grandmother and a little boy of two, a couple of cows
and a lot of chickens.

We are quite happy until the Hun begins to shell. Then
madame and her supporters vanish into the cellar and I
go for a short, but brisk walk.

With much love from your ever loving brother

Robert

Robert enjoyed a week of home leave in England during the summer of 1917. In her memoirs, Eileen described the excitement of being allowed two days off school to see him in London. The whole family went out to dinner and to see a show at the theatre. Eileen wrote in her memoirs, "It was wonderful seeing Bob again. He looked very handsome in his uniform…"

The next month the family heard that Bob (Robert) had been awarded the Military Cross medal for bravery. This is a reproduction of the citation that came with the medal.

Awarded the Military Cross.

Lieutenant Robert Edward Watson SEMPLE,
R.A., attached "Y" Guards Trench Mortar Battery.

_____

For bravery and devotion to duty while in command of a Trench Mortar Battery, during the operations, Donns and in Flanders. During the preparations for the attack on the 31st July he carried out all his allotted tasks in spite of destructive hostile fire which repeatedly buried his mortars.

_____

The main task of the mortar batteries on 31 July 1917 was to destroy the lines of German barbed wire protecting their front line trenches before the British soldiers attacked.

Robert received the Military Cross, one of five awards for bravery. These are: the Victoria Cross, the Distinguished Service Order, the Military Cross, the Distinguished Conduct Medal and the Military Medal.

Robert wrote his sisters a joint letter in September 1917 in which he described his living quarters. He was camping out in a French pub, an 'estaminet', which had been shelled and partly wrecked.

8th Sept 1917

My dearest Mabel and Eileen,

This letter is written from an "Estaminet", which is the French for Pub, which is the English for a house where one gets a glass of beer for a penny.

At present I am living here, but I dare not tell you its real name for fear the Germans should get to know, so to deceive them I will call it the "Crown Hotel".

Inside the Crown we have four large rooms with tiled floors. All their ceilings have been pulled down, and all the rooms above have been pulled down, so that you can look right up to the sky through the roof.

One of the front rooms has been covered in with a big tarpaulin. This is our mess, where we eat and drink. In the other front room there is a dugout covered all over with sandbags where I sleep. In one of the back rooms the servants cook. In the other nothing exciting ever happens because half of its outside walls have collapsed.

We stand by the side of a little road, and all around us are big shell holes.

And now, if you can picture me eating and drinking and going to bed and getting up again, you have a good idea of my life at present.

Give my love to all at home,
and I hope you are having a good time.

With much love from your ever loving brother
Robert.

P.S. I am bursting with health
and good spirits (not whiskey).

Robert writes that his dugout is well protected by sandbags. Bags filled with sand were piled up on top of each other to provide protection against shell blasts and enemy fire.

Robert, like so many soldiers during the First World War, makes light of his difficult living conditions when writing letters home. All the fighting and exploded shells created a devastated landscape with ruined buildings, huge craters and bare tree stumps. To get an idea of the area, you could look at official photographs or paintings, including those by one of the official war artists, Paul Nash.

On 13 October Robert had time to write a letter to both of his sisters and tells them similar news. He is worried about the danger that they might be in at boarding school in Ealing because of German air raids reported in a newspaper he has read. Some families sent out newspapers, which were passed around for all to read. Often soldiers learnt more about the progress of the war from reading the out-of-date newspapers than they did from being in the middle of the fighting.

13th Oct 1917.

My dearest Mabel,
Thank you so much for your letter. I can see from the papers that you get a lot of air raids. I do hope they keep clear of Ealing, for it would be no fun if they came too close.

A bomb dropped just outside my dugout the other night. Luckily it was quite a small one, and in any case we are well sandbagged in. I think that the last time I wrote to you I was living in a tent. At present I am stopping in the two remaining rooms of a house. They are well padded, but the great advantage is a big open fireplace, which will burn anything we care to put on it.

The weather is very bad. Nearly every day it rains, so all the country is covered with mud once more.

I am in very good health.

The other evening I had an awful accident.

I was sitting in the mess when I suddenly smelt something burning. After a short while I went round to my dugout to discover that a candle, which I had left burning by my bed, had set fire to all my blankets.

By good luck nothing much was burned except one or two shirts, and, as my winter clothes are on the way out, I will be able to make up the loss.

Mother and Father wrote to me last from Southsea. I hope they are not getting very bad weather down there.

With much love from your loving brother

Robert.

Robert has heard about German air raids on Britain. The first German air raids used a Zeppelin airship to drop bombs on coastal towns in December 1914. By 1917 they were using aeroplanes that could travel further over Britain. During 1917 and 1918 there were 27 air raids in Britain, causing 835 deaths and over 1,900 injuries.

By October 1917, Robert had just had his 21st birthday and Eileen her 15th. As usual, Robert tries to make his sister laugh by repeating the story about accidentally setting fire to his belongings which he also wrote about in his letter to Mabel (above). He does add that he is not enjoying himself at all.

13th Oct 1917

My dearest Eileen,

Here's to your good health and above all don't work too hard. Thanks very much for your letter. I am in very good health and not enjoying myself at all.

The weather is so wet. There is mud everywhere.

Our mess leaks like a sieve but thank goodness we have a nice big fireplace. This makes up for everything else. The other day I set fire to my kit. By good luck I only burned some shirts, and, as my winter shirts are on the way out, this will not matter.

The moral is "Do not set fire to your clothes".

The air raids must be quite exciting, but I hope they don't come too near.

The Hun dropped one of his eggs near our dugout the other night when he was flying over. We did not like it at all. However we feel quite safe because we are well sandbagged in.

Write again soon.

With much love from your loving brother
Robert

Robert mentions that a German aircraft flew over recently and dropped "his eggs", shells or bombs, close by. At the beginning of the war aeroplanes were mostly used to observe, look for details of what each side were doing. They also set out to destroy barrage balloons. These were tethered to the ground and were used to spy on enemy trenches. By 1917 aircraft were still being used to provide information about enemy positions but they were also fighting each other in the skies above the battlefields and dropping shells on the trenches, usually aiming for gun batteries or machine gun emplacements.

Robert writes that he is not enjoying himself: "The weather is so wet. There is mud everywhere." At this point he was taking part in the Third Battle of Ypres, also called Passchendaele. Thousands of soldiers lost their lives during this long battle fought in terribly wet weather. The landscape turned to mud and wounded men drowned in shell holes full of water.

57

This is the envelope that contained Robert's next letter to Mabel. Posted in France at a field post office, it was checked by a censor at one of the army post office depots on the French coast. The censor's job was to make sure that soldiers had not written anything that could be useful to the Germans, or write about war events that could make people at home feel too dismayed or disheartened. It joined other letters in one of the 19,000 mailbags that crossed the English Channel in 1917 before entering the normal British postal service.

15th Nov. 1917

My dearest Mabel aussi Eileen,
This photo which I send you represents me, and the other officers in the Trench Mortars.

The big officer on the top is called H. Taylor. On my right is 2/Lt Church. On my left is 2/Lt Byrne. Behind us is a fine old background very much the worse for wear.

The photo was taken in a town behind the lines. The studio was an old broken down conservatory.

I am in very good health but I am afraid I cannot write a long letter on account of the time.

Well! Here's the best of health.

Your loving brother
Robert.

Robert had visited a photographic studio with his friends to have their photo taken. Soldiers often had photos taken in studios in France or in Britain when they were on leave. They sent copies to their families, sometimes in the form of a picture postcard.

Robert asks Mabel to buy a cane weekend case in this next letter, possibly as a shared birthday gift from them to their mother. Mabel must have described a recent visit to Kew Gardens, the botanical gardens in London, in her latest letter to her brother. She was 16 by now and experimenting with her hairstyle.

18th Nov. 1917

My dearest Mabel,

I have no idea how much a cane weekend case costs, and I cannot very well send you any money from here unless I send you a cheque which I would have to send through Mother. Please get as good a one as you can. The more it costs the better. I expect to get a leave soon then I can help you out with it.

The best of luck to Lucy Hobson. You seem to have a good time at Kew. I remember Kew very well. I dare say you look well with your hair up, but then you see I am getting quite a dare devil.

Got it Steve?

Say stranger – guess I get your story.

See the effect America has on the War.

Your loving brother
Robert.

Robert finishes this letter in an American accent! The United States had joined the war on the British and French side in April 1917. It took a while for their troops to reach France and other war zones but when they did get into action, their presence helped to lift the spirits of the French and British troops and eventually became an important factor in winning the war in 1918.

Robert is possibly poking fun at some of the more out-dated weapons that soldiers still used in the First World War in this next letter, addressed to both of his sisters. As an officer, he had a sword and he has invented a shield to go with it in his sketch. The fat German soldier is shown bringing down a huge trench axe. In the second sketch Robert shows a German wearing a bear-skin hat and holding a lance.

At the beginning of the war, soldiers mounted on horseback (the cavalry) fought several battles. Most of the cavalry carried swords but some of them, the Lancers, carried a lance. Once trench warfare became established, mounted soldiers were very much in danger from machine gun fire. As a result, they were not used much although they did play their part during the Battle of the Somme in 1916. For most of the war, soldiers in cavalry units fought on foot, alongside other soldiers.

24th Nov. 1917

My dearest Mabel and Eileen,

(I insist on writing to both of you at once)

Oh happy day! – unlimited gratitude!
A letter from your noble brother who is fighting the
Germans in France.

I am writing you this letter during a few spare moments
in the fray. Seated on a cannon ball with my sword
stuck in the ground by my side. It is getting very
blunt. I shall have to clean it tomorrow morning. The
Crown Prince is seated within a biscuit's toss. He carries
a lance, but I will wait till I have finished this letter
before we join in mortal combat. –

You will see the result in the newspaper.

It is very cold out here at present. For the last two days there has been a very strong wind blowing. We have a little stove in our mess which we keep well supplied with wood. Our mess is a half round hut like this –

Our mess

"Pask" the mess waiter

Note the holes which the wind blew in our windows. I am in good health.

With much love from your loving brother
Robert.

Robert draws Pask, the mess waiter, running along carrying hot food for the officers. The officers' mess was where officers ate their meals and relaxed. Ordinary soldiers acted as their servants. The officers' mess shown in the drawing is a Nissen hut, designed during the war by Major Nissen. At least 100,000 were made during the war. Easy to put up and take down, they were ideal buildings for an army that was on the move.

Robert wrote to both of his sisters on 22 December 1917. They must have been relieved to receive their letters and hear that their brother and his company were out of the trenches in a rest camp for Christmas. Coping with cold weather made most soldiers miserable during the winter months. As usual, Robert is very brave about it in order not to worry his sisters.

22nd Dec. 1917

My dearest Mabel,

Are you having awfully cold weather? We are all nearly frozen out. There is about an inch of snow on the ground and every night, and most of the day, it freezes hard.

Luckily we are in good billets. We live in a camp of huts on the side of a hill just above a village. We are amongst a lot of trees, and the camp looks very pretty on these bright moonlight nights. The inside of our mess hut is covered with green canvas. It has a good fireplace in it, so it is very snug. I dare say Mother would say it was a bit stuffy.

We are arranging to have a good spread for Xmas. A big turkey has been bought. We have two puddings and a good supply of wine – so we should not do so badly.

Two pigs have been bought and killed for the men. They have a ration of plum pudding on Xmas day.

Please let me know how your play goes off.

I see from the paper that there was another raid on London. You must have just got home in time. What a good thing. This is just a short note to wish you a happy Xmas etc, but I am afraid it will arrive rather late.

I hope you had a good time when I was on leave.

With much love
from your loving brother
Robert.

For Robert's men, this was the first year that they were given plum pudding, another name for Christmas pudding, as part of their rations. Each man received half a pound of pudding in late December 1917. The fighting continued over the Christmas period so those in the front line would have taken it in turns to eat it.

Robert had just returned from home leave when he wrote this letter and the one above. Officers received more home leave than ordinary soldiers, who might have just one home leave per year. He again makes light of how cold it is in his living quarters (billets). At the end he asks her to send his love to the two little boys who had joined the Semple household earlier in the year – Sammy (Sam) and Tom.

22nd Dec. 1917

My dearest Eileen,
A happy Xmas, a bright New Year, and anything else you can think of.

I am back safe and sound with the mortars. We are in good billets. I would describe them, but I have already done it once in Mabel's letter. Everything is frozen hard.

The butter has to be placed on the stove, and my sponge is like a brick every morning. I do hope your play goes off well.

I had a very nice comfortable journey back from England, much better than I expected.

A French officer has been staying at our mess. He is an interpreter. Last night we gave him a farewell dinner as he had to leave us. He was a very good fellow, and he had a beard.

I am writing this letter on the tablecloth I bought for the mess in London.

Give my love to Sammy and Tom.

With much love from
your loving brother

Robert.

Robert mentions a French interpreter in this letter. With the British and the French armies fighting on the same side, interpreters were vital to translate officers' battle ideas and plans.

~ **1918** ~

By now, countries that had been fighting since August 1914 were short of money, supplies and, most importantly, food. The German army commanders needed a quick victory and planned a big push forward. In March and April, German troops broke through the British and French front line in several places. Soon they were 64 km (40 miles) from Paris.

Then it all started to go wrong for the exhausted German troops as, once again, the war ground to a halt. They had gained some land but at the cost of a great number of soldiers' lives. Between May and August, the German army made no more progress. In the meantime, American troops and equipment were adding strength to the British, French and Allied armies. On 8 August, these armies attacked along much of the German front line. Success was now on the side of the Allies, whose troops were supported by tanks, aircraft and artillery.

On 8 August, the Allies used battle tactics that had been developed over the previous years of war. Robert Semple, and those who fought in the Royal Artillery, had new equipment that allowed them to hit German gun positions with much greater accuracy. In addition, the artillery had become much better at creating a battle tactic called the creeping barrage. This allowed troops to attack across No Man's Land protected by a curtain of shells fired by the artillery. The guns fired the shells further and further across No Man's Land as the troops walked forward, protecting them from German gunfire.

The fighting continued through September and October and eventually the British army and her allies marched into Germany. Sadly, 260,000 British soldiers were killed or injured during the last hundred days of the war. It became clear that the German government needed a peace settlement. The fighting stopped at 11 o'clock in the morning of 11 November.

In March 1918, Robert signed his letter to Eileen as Robert (Capt). He had been promoted! As a captain in the artillery, he was in charge of his trench mortar battery.

10-3-18

My dearest Eileen,
I really would have written to you before, but I have really been busy this time.

I was very pleased to get your letters.

I am trays beans which is the Anglo-French for Très bien [very well].

Please do not do anything dreadful to get another smack.

It only remains for me to sign myself your ever loving brother, Robert (Capt)

This is an aeroplane (rather good)

Look at these – 3 of them

The rank of captain was shown by three stars sewn onto the shoulder straps or the cuffs of the army tunic, as Robert has drawn. His official army portrait shows the same.

In this next letter, Robert writes, "I am busy just now hurling the H.E. at the Hun." The H.E. he was hurling at the Hun (Germans) stood for high explosive shells. Although he reassures Mabel that he is quite safe, the cottage where he lives has recently been shelled by the Germans.

14th April

My dearest Mabel,

In case you are worrying about me – I am quite safe and sound. Give sister Eileen my best wishes. Tell her that if I feel strong enough at the end of this letter I shall probably write to her, but the odds are that my intellect will collapse long before I am half way through.

I am busy just now hurling the H.E. at the Hun. We have dug in our mortars and have quite a jolly time till the Hun gets annoyed, then we hide in holes and pretend it wasn't us.

Oh it's the life –

I live in a shack about a mile or so to the rear. We have our mess in a little cottage. It used to look quite pretty, but a day or two ago it got a direct hit on the roof which rather spoilt the effect.

We saved a piano out of a hut near the line and brought it down to the mess on a handcart.

Some of the notes are missing and a good many of the wires were broken. However we banged her about and tied knots in the wires and now we whack any old tune out of her.

Camouflage is all the rage out here. My gunpits look like nothing on earth and I am expert at disguising myself as a lump of dirt – by lying flat on the ground. I give this performance on and off most of the day and several times during the night.

I really forget how Easter holidays run, but I imagine you should be at St Swithan just now.

If so give my love to everyone at home, and take my very best love.

Your loving brother
Robert.

Robert and his gun battery were clearly busy in April 1918. On 21 March, the German army launched a carefully planned attack on the Western Front. After a huge bombardment – three million shells were fired in three hours – German soldiers pushed forward. In just a week, the German army managed to advance 60 kilometres (40 miles). In April they were still keeping up the attacks.

Camouflage became increasingly necessary as the war progressed in order to protect the guns from German aircraft flying overhead. Robert writes that his gunpits "look like nothing on earth". They would have been covered in a large net, threaded through with branches and leaves.

Despite the difficulties of his day-to-day life, Robert reminds his sister Eileen to practise her piano in April 1918. In this letter and the one above Robert shows that his fun spirit is still there. With his friends, he has moved a broken down piano by using a handcart, which can't have been easy since pianos are very heavy.

15 April

My dearest Eileen

Just the smallest note to let you know that I am quite well and to send you my love. I hope you are having good weather for your holidays. Do not forget to practise your piano.

By the way I am getting a lot of fun out of a funny collection of wood and wire which we choose to call a piano.

Hang out all your flags and to H– with the Hun.

With best love from your loving brother
Robert.

In May 1918, Mabel was reaching the end of her school years. Her parents must have been discussing her future and Robert has heard about her plans in one of the letters from home. Robert sounds tired in this letter. He has been at war for three years with only a few breaks back in England on leave.

16th May 1918

Dearest Mabel,

I had thought of writing to you in verse, but the day is so hot and I feel so limp, that I thought better of it. Really, I got as far as

>"Dearest Mabel
>
>If you're able
>
>For to listen to my song"

but after that my mind went blank, although I sat a long time with a pencil in my hand looking at the paper (I believe they call it "courting the muse").

Thank you for your letter. I wish I could have functioned in your play if only as the scene shifter.

Did it have scenery or was it one of the very advanced plays?

I hear that you are leaving school soon. Let me know what you think of it – After that I gather you are going to learn typewriting, shorthand, sewing, window cleaning, ploughing, first aid, and carpet beating – very useful indeed – very useful.

But joking apart I hope you take up some work that you are interested in.

At present I am resting from the fatigue of war in a small dirty village behind the lines.

The spring has come and hidden all the dirt, only occasionally one can smell it – Still it is very beautiful.

This morning I have spent lying in a field with my coat and shirt off having a sun bath. Sounds nice doesn't it?

I am getting quite fat on fresh eggs and milk.

We can get a lot of those here. Eggs are 4d each which I think is very dear "mais c'est la guerre". That is French for but otherwise no profit could be made out of the hard-working English soldier.

Before I came out for this rest I had been in action from Jan. without a break during which time I accounted for several little Hunlets all smaller than myself.

Think of me out at the Great War lying on my back in an orchard smoking a cigarette. If the Germans come I have decided to cover myself with grass and pretend I'm a haystack.

With my very very best love from your loving brother
Robert

Robert writes that he has been in action since January, killing German soldiers (Hunlets) by firing shells at their trenches and probably shooting them during trench raids. Robert's location on the Western Front meant that he was in great danger at this time as the Germans seemed to be winning.

Thousands of British soldiers died in the spring of 1918. Thousands more were taken prisoner by the Germans. As usual, because he is writing to his younger sister, he tries to make light of the horrors of war. Reading between the lines, he sounds pretty fed up with his life.

Robert uses the term 'the Great War' which was how everyone referred to the First World War until the Second World War (1939 to 1945).

Two days later he wrote a letter to Eileen. During this rest time, Robert found a peaceful place to write this letter – an apple orchard.

18th May 1918

My dearest Eileen,

I am sitting in a small orchard under the shade of an apple tree.

The orchard is shut off by a very tall green hedge.

It is beautifully warm and peaceful.

If you could see me you would think I was anywhere but three quarters of an hour's walk from the German trenches.

I am living on the fat of the land at present – Eating, drinking (milk?) and sleeping.

Absolutely nothing to worry about, except a stray bomb or two dropped during the night, but then you know how careless these German flying men are.

When I have finished this letter I am going to make a hammock out of a piece of sacking and go to sleep in it.

What a long long war it is – If I don't get my leave soon I shall send in my resignation.

That would help to hurry matters one way or the other.

Believe me I would write you a longer letter if I could keep awake.

With lots and lots of love from your loving brother, Robert

Robert jokes with his sister that if he doesn't get home leave soon he will send in his resignation. Of course he was not allowed to do that – and if he had walked away from his position in the army, he could have been shot as a deserter.

It seems as if Robert still hadn't had leave by the time he wrote this letter two and a half months later. He has heard about Eileen catching Hun (German) measles. Her memoirs mention this illness, which stopped her from performing as a lion in a performance of Shakespeare's *A Midsummer Night's Dream*. She had made herself "a wonderful tail which I had wired and could move about in an amusing manner".

1st Aug 1918

My dearest Mabel,

This letter ought to reach you just before you break up for the holidays. I do hope Eileen has recovered sufficiently from her attack of Hun measles for her to go home. It would be poor sport if she had to wait behind.

No doubt you are wondering where I got this fine notepaper from. It is quite sufficient to know that I bought it.

Oh I am very cheerful and in fine health.

My leave has faded into the background again. I do not know when I shall get it.

I have practically nothing to say. Give my love to anyone you think should have it and keep as much as you like for yourself.

From your loving brother

Robert.

Many men, including Robert, had their leave cancelled in August. The French and the British armies were planning a big push forward. The German army's successes of earlier in the year had faded away. Now, with the US troops fighting alongside the British, Commonwealth and French troops, the Germans suffered many defeats in September and October and were gradually pushed back towards Germany.

The descendants of Mabel and Eileen only have one surviving letter written by Robert to the children's mother – Lady Ethel. Her husband, Sir David, had finished his job in Egypt and was back in England. It seems as if Robert finally had some leave to visit his family. Robert writes that he is terribly pleased with the parcel of food (rations) and magazines that he has received from his parents. He reassures his mother that he is cleaning his teeth and washing his face when he can. It wasn't easy to keep clean in the trenches.

8th Sept 1918

My dearest Mother,
Your letter reached me last night with the rations.

You can imagine how pleased I was. We had been sitting in this dugout all day with nothing very much to do except to keep a bright look out on the Hun. We were bored stiff in fact when I got your letter and a big parcel of magazines from Father.

During the last few days we have had a fairly busy time. Yesterday morning I had my first wash for four days. I cleaned my teeth, shaved, and washed my face and hands in a cup full of water. Water is scarce and we cannot afford to use it for washing. I do like looking back on the good time I had on leave. It helps to make you brighter not to think of the present too much.

I have just finished stand to in the morning which takes place roughly from four to five or six.

This is the best time in the day during this hot weather. I do hope it keeps fine for your holiday, and that you have a very good time.

With very very much love from your loving son
Robert.

Robert wrote this letter early in the morning after the 'stand to', the stand-to-arms. All along the front line, soldiers stood with their rifles ready, on the alert for possible German attacks, most likely in the weak light of dawn. Sentries continued to keep a sharp watch for any movement across No Man's Land throughout the day. At the end of the day there was the 'stand down' where a similar routine was followed.

The rest of the time, soldiers in the front line settled down to their usual activities. Boredom was a big problem, as Robert mentions here: "We were bored stiff in fact when I got your letter and a big parcel of magazines from Father." At any moment a German shell might land close by or they might have to defend the front line from a surprise attack, but they often had little to do. They spent their time repairing the trench, cleaning equipment, writing letters, taking naps, preparing snacks, smoking cigarettes and sharing magazines.

In October 1918, Eileen fell ill with Spanish flu (influenza). So many girls caught the flu at her school that they turned it into a hospital, bringing in nursing staff to help with the sick. Eileen was ill for most of that autumn. During 1918 and 1919 the flu would kill 40 million people worldwide.

Then, the Semple family had another member of the family to worry about. They received news that Robert had been wounded on 22 October. Gunshot wounds across his thigh and leg landed him in hospital in Rouen, northern France. However, his wounds were not considered serious and he was expected to recover.

Much later on, Mabel told her children that she had a horrible dream at this time in which the family were mourning Robert (Bob's) death. She pleaded with her father to set off for France to check that her brother was receiving the best care and attention. Soon after, a telegram arrived urging the family to come quickly if they wanted to see Robert alive.

Sir David set off for France to check on his son's recovery. On arrival, he discovered that Robert had caught the Spanish flu and was fighting for his life. Despite his medical training, Robert's father could do nothing to help his son. Robert died on 5 November 1918, aged 22.

Six days later,
the war came to an end.

Worn out by months of losses,
German leaders signed a peace
agreement and both sides
agreed to stop fighting at
11 am on 11 November 1918.

William Semple is buried at Hannescamps New Military Cemetery, Pas-de Calais, France. When he died he was buried by German soldiers, his grave marked by a wooden cross bearing his name. At some point his grave was moved. The cemetery where he is buried was begun in March 1916 and contains 102 burials and commemorations. Most of the burials took place during the war but 30 graves were moved there after the war ended in 1918. It is likely that William was one of those since the address given for his parents, inscribed on the gravestone, is where they were living after the war.

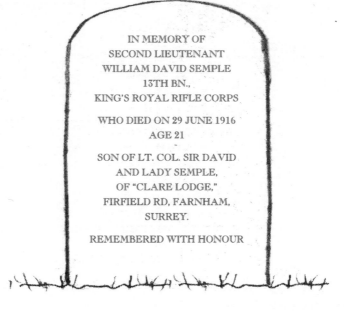

IN MEMORY OF
SECOND LIEUTENANT
WILLIAM DAVID SEMPLE
13TH BN.,
KING'S ROYAL RIFLE CORPS

WHO DIED ON 29 JUNE 1916
AGE 21

SON OF LT. COL. SIR DAVID
AND LADY SEMPLE,
OF "CLARE LODGE,"
FIRFIELD RD, FARNHAM,
SURREY.

REMEMBERED WITH HONOUR

Robert Semple is buried at St Sever Cemetery Extension, Rouen, France. The hospital in Rouen where Robert died cared for wounded soldiers all through the war and there were several other hospitals in the town. As a result, the town cemetery filled up quickly and this extension to it was begun in September 1916. In all 8,348 First World War soldiers are buried there.

IN MEMORY OF
CAPTAIN ROBERT
EDWARD WATSON SEMPLE MC
ROYAL FIELD ARTILLERY

WHO DIED ON
5 NOVEMBER 1918 AGE 22

SON OF SIR DAVID SEMPLE, LT,
R.A.M.C. & LADY SEMPLE OF
7 HIGH PARK GARDENS, KEW,
SURREY.

WAS ENGAGED FOR
THREE YEARS AND THREE
MONTHS IN THE FIGHTING
LINE IN FRANCE.
REMEMBERED WITH HONOUR

WAR GRAVES

Almost a million men in the British armed forces died during the war. After the war, the Imperial War Graves Commission (now the Commonwealth War Graves Commission) had an enormous task to complete. It built over a thousand cemeteries in France and Belgium alone. The bodies of many dead soldiers were reburied in these cemeteries, each grave marked by a simple wooden cross, eventually changed to a stone gravestone. Where it was impossible to identify a soldier's body, it was marked by a gravestone engraved with 'A SOLDIER OF THE GREAT WAR' or 'A BRITISH SOLDIER OF THE GREAT WAR' and the words 'KNOWN UNTO GOD'.

Those soldiers who have no known grave are remembered on stone memorials to the missing, including the Menin Gate at Ypres in Belgium. Over 50,000 names are listed on this memorial by name and regiment. Each evening since 1929 (except for a short time during the Second World War), local bugle players sound out the 'Last Post' to commemorate the soldiers who lost their lives close to Ypres.

WAR MEMORIALS

With the bodies of loved ones laid to rest abroad, many people felt a great need for a war memorial in their own community. People formed committees and raised money to build war memorials in churches, on village greens and on high streets. Some built memorial gardens or even swimming pools. William and Robert are remembered in several places:

✳ on a plaque inside St Michael's Church, Woburn Sands, where their family lived during the war;

✳ on a memorial in Campbell College school hall, Belfast, where they both went to school;

✳ on the war memorial in the graveyard of St Saviour's Church, St Alban's, where the family were living in 1917 to 1918.

William's name also appears alongside other students of Clare College, Cambridge who died in the First World War. Their names are engraved in the arch that forms the entrance to Memorial Court, built as a memorial to those who had died in the First World War. In addition, William's name appears on the war memorial inside Clare College Chapel.

Robert and all who served with the Royal Artillery are commemorated on the monument unveiled in Hyde Park, London in 1925:

IN PROUD REMEMBRANCE
OF THE FORTY-NINE THOUSAND
& SEVENTY-SIX
OF ALL RANKS OF
THE ROYAL REGIMENT OF ARTILLERY
WHO GAVE THEIR LIVES
FOR KING AND COUNTRY
IN THE GREAT WAR
1914—1919.

There are several war memorials around the country to the men of the King's Royal Rifle Corps, William's regiment.

THE SEMPLE FAMILY
AFTER THE WAR

Alongside millions of families across Europe, the Semple family had to learn to live with great loss and sadness. In 1922 Sir David applied for the medals due to his sons for having fought in the war: the Star Medal, British War Medal and the Victory Medal.

In the 1920s Mabel asked everyone to call her by her middle name, Katherine. She trained and worked as an artist, married, had four children and became a children's book illustrator. Her youngest son is called William Robert Brian after her brothers and her husband. When she married in 1928, she ran across from the bridal party, gathered outside St Saviour's Church, St Alban's, to place her wedding bouquet on the war memorial inscribed with her brothers' names.

Eileen, also known as Jelly, trained as a nurse when she first left home but decided to emigrate to Canada in 1922, maybe to escape the sadness of her parents. She worked in many different jobs, married for a short while and returned to England finally in 1937 when her father was seriously ill. She spent the rest of her life in England, married again but did not have children.

Maud, the shadowy eldest sister in this story, became a nun and took the name Sister Mary David. She went on to be Reverent Mother of the Order of the Sacred Heart and died at the great age of 98.

Much more recently, Mabel's children discovered that Sam Lawrence, the small boy brought home by Lady Ethel in 1917, was probably their Uncle William's illegitimate son. Sam was brought up by the Semples and set up in business but he wasn't told that he was their grandson. It isn't clear whether Sir David knew of this possible family link.

A sketch of her youngest son, Bill, by Katherine (Mabel) Wigglesworth.

ARMISTICE DAY

Eleven o'clock in the morning on 11 November became the time when the whole country stopped their lives to remember those who had died during the war. This continues today.

In 1920 King George V unveiled the stone monument called the Cenotaph at Whitehall in central London, the ultimate war memorial to those who had died during the war. That same year the body of an unnamed soldier was buried in the grave of the Unknown Warrior, Westminster Abbey.

THE POPPY

The first British Legion Poppy Day was held in the run up to Armistice Day in 1921. Volunteers sold red silk poppies to raise money that was used to help men who had served in the war and were in need, or their families. It became a tradition for people to wear the poppies each year.

The poppy was one of the first flowers to spring up in soil disturbed by battles or burials along the Western Front. For this reason, poppies are mentioned in several poems written at this time, including 'In Flanders Fields' by Canadian army doctor, John McCrae. Here are the first five lines:

> In Flanders fields the poppies blow
> Between the crosses, row on row,
> That mark our place; and in the sky
> The larks, still bravely singing, fly
> Scarce heard amid the guns below.

FIRST WORLD WAR TIMELINE

Important dates relating to the First World War, especially the Western Front.

1914

28 June – Archduke Franz Ferdinand is assassinated
28 July – Austria-Hungary declares war on Serbia
1 August – Germany declares war on Russia
3 August – Germany declares war on France
4 August – Britain declares war on Germany
23–25 August – Battle of Mons/Battle of Le Cateau
6–12 September – Battle of the Marne
September–November – Trenches dug by both sides
19 October–17 November – First Battle of Ypres
25 December – Peace along certain sections of the Western Front

1915

19 January – First air raid on Britain (Great Yarmouth)
24 January – Battle of Dogger Bank (naval battle)
25 April – British and Allied troops land at Gallipoli
22 April–25 May – Second Battle of Ypres – first use of poison gas
25–28 September – Battle of Loos

1916

25 January – An Act of Parliament makes all single men between 18 and 41 eligible for conscription
21 February–31 August – Battle of Verdun
31 May – Battle of Jutland (naval battle)
1 July–18 November – Battle of the Somme

1917

12 March – Start of the Russian Revolution
6 April – The USA declares war on Germany
9 April–15 May – Battle of Arras
31 July–10 November – Third Battle of Ypres (Passchendaele)
December – Peace agreed between the Russians and the Germans
20 November–7 December – Battle of Cambrai

1918

3 March – Russia signs peace treaty with Germany
March/April/May – German army successes along the Western Front
1 April – The Royal Air Force is created
18 July–5 August – Second Battle of the Marne / German army starts to collapse
8 August – Britain and her allies launch a series of attacks along the Western Front
11 November – The Armistice is signed and the war officially ends

GLOSSARY

Allies – the countries which fought alongside Britain and France during the First World War. Britain, France, Russia (until 1917), Australia, Canada, Newfoundland, New Zealand, South Africa, India (including Pakistan, Bangladesh and Sri Lanka) and others fought Germany, Austria-Hungary and Turkey (the Central Powers) and Bulgaria

Artillery – field guns and trench mortars

Billet – accommodation for troops

B.E.F. – short for British Expeditionary Force

Bugle – a small trumpet

Captain – an officer (above Lieutenant and below Major)

Cenotaph – the war memorial in central London, unveiled in 1920. 'Cenotaph' means 'empty tomb' in Greek

Censor – someone whose job it was to read soldiers' letters or other communications to check for information that could be useful to the enemy, or harmful to the general public

Commonwealth – the group of countries that support each other (and were once part of the British Empire) including Australia, Canada, India, Pakistan, South Africa, New Zealand, the UK and Jamaica

Dugout – an underground room cut into the side of a trench

Entrenched – dug in, well-established

Firing line – the front line of the trench system

Governess – a woman employed to teach children at home

Great War – the words used to describe the First World War until the Second World War

Gun battery – four or eight guns and the men that were trained to operate them

Gun emplacement – platform on which the guns were placed

Hun – soldiers' slang for a German soldier

Illegitimate – a child born to a mother who isn't married

John Peel – a popular 19th century song with the first line: *D'ye ken John Peel*

King's Royal Rifle Corps – one of the British army's infantry regiments

No Man's Land – the area of ground between the two opposing lines of trenches

Observation post – a place such as a ruined house or tree, used by a soldier to spy on the enemy's movements

Postal orders – a form of voucher, which was a safe way for parents or others to send money to men serving abroad

Royal Field Artillery – the part of the army responsible for the field guns and trench mortars

Second Lieutenant – a junior officer. In the army, he was usually in charge of between 25 and 40 men

Shell – a metal projectile filled with explosives and balls of lead (could also contain gas or smoke)

Sniper – a skilled marksman in the army

Sub – short for subaltern, a military word for a junior officer below the rank of captain, usually a second lieutenant

Tailor – someone who makes clothes to fit individual customers

Trench – a deep ditch in the ground used to provide protection for soldiers, sometimes built up with sandbags to provide more shelter

Trench mortar – a type of weapon developed during the war to suit trench warfare. It consisted of a short tube designed to fire a shell at a steep angle so that it fell down onto the enemy close by in the opposing trenches

Western Front – the zone of fighting stretching between the North Sea coast in Belgium, through France to the Swiss border

INDEX